Anonymous

The American Union Commission

Anonymous

The American Union Commission

ISBN/EAN: 9783744732017

Printed in Europe, USA, Canada, Australia, Japan

Cover: Foto ©ninafisch / pixelio.de

More available books at **www.hansebooks.com**

THE
AMERICAN UNION COMMISSION

SPEECHES

OF

Hon. W. Dennison, Postmaster-General,
Rev. J. P. Thompson, D.D., President of the Commission,
Col. N. G. Taylor, of East Tennessee,
Hon. J. R. Doolittle, U. S. Senate,
Gen. J. A. Garfield, M. C.,

IN THE

HALL OF REPRESENTATIVES,

WASHINGTON, FEB. 12, 1865.

New York:
PRINTED BY SANFORD, HARROUN & CO., STEAM PRINTING HOUSE, 644 BROADWAY.

1865.

WASHINGTON CITY, January 18, 1865.

Rev. Dr. J. P. Thompson, President of the American Union Commission, New York:

DEAR SIR :—Believing that the object of your Commission should be better understood by Congress, the people here, and throughout our country generally ; and in order to beget a more practical sympathy and suitable action, in aid of the many poor white refugees of the South, we would respectfully invite you to deliver a public address in this city on the subject.

Respectfully yours, &c.,

GEORGE W. JULIAN, M. C.
F. C. LE BLOND, M. C.
JOHN WILSON, Third Auditor.
THOS. CORWIN, Ex. Gov. of Ohio.
WM. JOHNSON, Esq., of Ohio.
JOHN W. FINNELL, Esq., of Ky.
P. D. GURLEY, D. D.
HON. PETER PARKER,
LORIN BLODGET, Esq.
FREDERICK N. KNAPP, U. S. S. Com.
WM. BALLANTYNE, Christian Com.

Notes of invitation were also sent by the Hon. W. Dennison, Hon. John Sherman, Hon. J. M. Edmunds, and Rev. J. C. Smith, D. D.

NEW YORK, January 26, 1865.

Hon. W. Dennison, Hon. John Sherman, Hon. G. W. Julian, Hon. F. C. Le Blond, Hon. J. M. Edmunds, Hon. John Wilson, Rev. Dr. P. D. Gurley, and others :

GENTLEMEN :—Accept my thanks for your courteous invitation to deliver an address in Washington, setting forth the objects of the American Union Commission.

It will afford me special pleasure to bring the work of the Commission to the knowledge of the citizens of Washington, and incidentally of members of Congress and of the National Government. The cause is not only humane and Christian, but patriotic and national.

Col. N. G. Taylor of East Tennessee, will represent the Commission with me, and we would designate Sabbath Evening, February 12th, for the purpose.

With high respect, your obd't serv't,

JOSEPH P. THOMPSON,
President American Union Commission.

In accordance with the foregoing invitation, a public meeting in behalf of the AMERICAN UNION COMMISSION was held in the hall of the House of Representatives, Washington, D. C., on Sunday evening, February 12, 1865. Hon. W. DENNISON, Postmaster General of the United States presided.

The exercises were opened with prayer by Rev. A. S. Fiske, lately a chaplain in the U. S. Army.

REMARKS OF HON. W. DENNISON.

The Chairman then said:

The *American Union Commission* has for its object the amelioration of the condition of loyalists, refugees from the South, who have sought an asylum from the calamities of the war, in the loyal states, and within the lines of our armies. It seeks to embrace in a single organization, the granting of relief to all who have been driven from their homes by the rebellion, and are in need of food and clothing, and who are without the means of supplying themselves with the necessaries of life. The Commission charges itself with the duty also of procuring employment for such of the refugees as are able to work, and making arrangements for establishing schools for the children who constitute a large proportion of the refugee population. To use the language of the fundamental article of the Commission, it is constituted " for the purpose of aiding and co-operating with the people of those portions of the United States which have been desolated and impoverished by the war, in the restoration of their civil and social condition, upon the basis of industry, education, freedom, and Christian morality."

Apprehending that the objects of the Commission, as well as the necessities of its organization, are not as well understood by the Government or the country as they should be, and impressed with the importance of having authentic information on the subject communicated to Congress and the people, a number of gentlemen, a few weeks since, invited the President of the Commission to deliver a public address in this city on the subject; and it gives me pleasure to inform you that he is present for that purpose, and will, with other gentlemen who have kindly consented to address you, explain fully the objects of the Commission, and the plans adopted for their accomplishment.

SPEECH OF REV. DR. THOMPSON.

Jos. P. Thompson, D.D., of New York, was then introduced. He said:

"Mr. President, I thank you for the lucid exposition which you have given of the principles, the objects, and the methods of the American Union Commission, and for the favorable introduction you have given it to this assembly.

The historian of this war will devote a very important chapter to the influence of the war in developing the philanthropy of the nation. Upon the one hand, indeed, when the veil is lifted awhile from the scenes of guerilla warfare, and from the prisons within the rebel lines, there are disclosed to us cruelties and barbarities that cause us to blush for American civilization, and which history will record with mingled incredulity and shame. But on the other hand, this war has developed, through all the loyal nation, a munificence of philanthropy without precedent in the history of Christianity itself. Had it been a war of aggression—were it a war of merely political interests, or for the aggrandizement of a party—were it a foreign war—a war of conquest—this might not have been. But this war touches the deepest springs of human thought and action, and leads us up step by step, under the manifest guidance of Divine Providence, to the highest moral issues. And, through this training, there has been a development of the philanthropy of the people upon the grandest scale.

No less than four distinct classes have been thrown directly upon our hands for sympathy and aid. First of all, our wounded and suffering soldiers on the field and in the hospital. The unanimous sentiment of the nation, is, that the men who are perilling all and suffering all for the country, deserve all at the hands of the people. The Sanitary Commission, which is one of the best exponents of practical Christianity, and the Christian Commission, which is one of the best exponents of the vital unity of the church of God—these two Commissions, ministering to the wants of the body, and to the comfort and peace of the soul, command, and I doubt not, will, till the close of the war, continue to command, the unanimous support of the loyal people of the nation.

Next to the soldiers, we have had thrown upon us an afflicted and outraged race, long down-trodden and oppressed, now rising to receive, not only sympathy and charity at our hands, but to receive justice, which, blessed be God, has been rendered to them within this very hall. But this people, who, for the time, have so large and so pressing a claim upon our resources, will, presently, I think, cease to demand charitable sympathy and aid. I have so much confidence in that wronged and abused race, in their essential manhood, in their facile character, their power of adaptation to new circumstances, contingencies and conditions, that I believe the time is not far distant when the black man (as was intimated by his eloquent representative in this place this morning)* will have as little need of special legislation as any class in the country. Give him his home, give him his family, give him the just wages of his labor, give him his rights as a citizen, and he will dispense with your tutelage, and cast off the feeling of dependence. Under the instincts of liberty he will show himself a man; and he who has taken care both of himself and his master, will assuredly take care of himself and of his own! What the black man should have at our hands is mainly the certainty of protection in his liberty; and for the rest, he may well be trusted to look out for himself.

A third class have been thrown upon us for our sympathy and aid, concerning whom I will speak but for a moment. I refer to the loyal occupants of portions of States in rebellion and within the theatre of war. For example, the people of West Virginia. West Virginia has put her full quota into the

* Rev. HENRY HIGHLAND GARNET had preached in the Hall of Representatives in the morning.

field for the defence of the nation under every call; and, I am
told, has not in a single instance resorted to the expedient
of substitutes and bounty-jumpers. Yet, an area of 16,000
miles of that State has been overrun by the two contending
armies not less than twelve times; the country has been
stripped bare of all the necessaries of life; and multitudes of
her population have been driven forth homeless, needing now
the hand of sympathy and of fraternal encouragement. A
careful computation by responsible persons in that State shows
that not less than ten thousand of its inhabitants, at this very
day, are in these necessitous circumstances, and must be helped
by us, not only through the winter, but through the coming
spring, in re-establishing their deserted homes.

Of East Tennessee, I shall not assume to speak. The loyalty
and fidelity of that region, the sufferings her people have
endured, and their present wants, will be set before you
to-night by my friend Col. Taylor, who will speak not only
with the eloquence of nature and of culture, but with the glow
of a martyr-patriotism, and the pathos of a suffering exile.
That people demand large sympathy at our hands, because
their sufferings have been greatly aggravated by our want of
sagacity and promptitude as a nation at the outset of the war.
I hesitate not to say that, had we then followed the sagacious
indications of two of the most sagacious men in these United
States—had we adopted the recommendation of the President of the United States, to build forthwith the railroad to
connect the Ohio River with Knoxville, and the equally sagacious demand of Gen. Sherman for 200,000 men as a force
with which to begin the war in Tennessee—depend upon it,
Sir, it would have cost us but one campaign to have extermin-
ated the rebellion from the soil of that State; and there would
have been no question here the other day as to whether there
was a State of Tennessee entitled to an electoral vote.—
[Applause.]

We owe everything to that brave people who have remained
true to our flag through manifold trials and sufferings. I said
to a loyal son of Tennessee, a few months ago, 'We of the

North have known nothing of trial, and suffering, and sacrifice in the cause of the country, in comparison with what you have endured ; and let me pledge you, sir, that when these days of peril and of blood are over, the people will remember you and such as you.' 'I am not indifferent,' was his manly answer, 'to the good-will of my fellow-citizens ; but I assure you, that has not been in my thoughts. I had a home ; I had a competence, the result of years of toil ; I had friends ; I had honors and offices, as many as I cared for or deserved. I lost all these ; but it was for my country ; and I have determined to sacrifice all for her sake, and to put down this accursed rebellion.' I could but repeat, 'Sir, you will not be forgotten.' And the nation redeemed that pledge when it said to him, on the eighth day of November, 'You, who have no home, shall now be adopted as the second citizen of the Republic ; you, who have no State shall sit under the dome of the National Capitol, presiding over the Senate of all the States.' [Applause.]

There is another class, Mr. President, whom I wish particularly to bring to the notice of this assembly, leaving to Col. Taylor the description of his friends in East Tennessee. I refer to that mixed multitude known properly as REFUGEES, who are stranded within our lines by the tides of war—homeless, friendless, penniless—driven out by their fears—driven out by threats—driven out by guerilla invasions—driven out by starvation—driven out now by the advance of rebel armies, and again by the order of our own commanders under military necessity.

As these people began to flow in upon Nashville, upon Memphis, and Vicksburg, and various points of military occupation at the South, the two Commissions already in the field, the Christian and the Sanitary, though restricted by their constitutions to the army and the navy, generously offered such relief as was at hand, under the dictates of humanity. But it was felt that they could not, in justice to the soldiers, assume the care of this vast and increasing number of impoverished people. Then the Government provided for them half rations, and to a limited extent, transportation. But there was a want of uniformity in policy, there was want of organization ; and the evil increased in magnitude. It is computed, that not less than 80,000 of this class of people have been thrown within our lines since the war began. It was a very uncertain calamity; we knew not at what quarter it would next break forth upon us. For example, when Nashville was threatened last fall, the Government, as a military necessity, ejected from that city some four or five thousand refugees, who were then there, and who were housed in barracks,—sending them on to Clarksville, Cairo and other places, in order that the buildings they had occupied might be used as hospitals for the soldiers. At the same time, the advance of Hood's army expelled other thousands from their homes; and within the period of a few days, not less than 5,000 were huddled together in Murfreesboro, awaiting transportation to Nashville, to take the place of those who had been sent beyond. Local charities were started to relieve this misery at various points, and special appeals were addressed to the people of the North in our principal cities. But still in this sudden emergency, as I have said, there was a want of uniform policy and organization, both among the people at large and with the Government.

To meet this state of facts—recognizing this as a vast national calamity, to be grappled with, with all the resources both of the Government and of popular charity—this Commission was called into existence. Its fundamental article has been read, and its principal object has been set before you by the Chairman. I am happy to say that at the very outset, the President of the United States was pleased to express his approval (which we possess in writing,) and to commend this organization to public favor. At the same time, the War Department very liberally granted to us all facilities consistent with military exigencies for prosecuting our work.

Our first endeavor was to systematize within one organization, the various local and spasmodic movements to which I have referred, to relieve this description of misery; and we have been so far successful, that, in addition to the principal

Commission, which is organized on the same basis as the Sanitary and the Christian Commissions—in addition to the principal Commission established in the City of New York, there is now a New England branch, represented at the City of Boston as its head quarters, with a very efficient Executive Committee there (the lamented Mr. Everett was its President); there is a branch at Cincinnati (in the hands of gentlemen who have had experience in both this and the Sanitary work), which will cover Ohio and adjacent States; there is a branch at Chicago, recently organized for the Northwest; and there are local agencies at Cairo, at Louisville, at Nashville, at Memphis, and at various other points where this distress exists. Moreover, my friend, Col. Taylor, proposes hereafter to carry forward his appeals for East Tennessee in connection with this organization; and the association for the relief of West Virginia will do the same.

We have thus simplified and nationalized this charity, which every one will see is a matter of great economy in respect to the distribution of funds and the working of appropriate agencies. Before I enter upon the specific details of the work, let me for a moment introduce you to this class of people and this description of suffering.

Could I take you for a single hour to the scenes that I witnessed in Nashville a few months ago, when on a visit to the army of Gen. Sherman, then in North-Western Georgia, every heart would upon the instant approve this movement as necessary and momentous. I entered a large building, once occupied as a medical college, and found in it at that time some 300 human beings, mostly women and children, the remnants of families, each little group clustering by itself; very poorly clad; most of them in rags; without any means of subsistence but the half-rations derived from the Government, altogether inappropriate and inadequate for the sick and the feeble; with no kind of superintendence; huddled together *en masse*; filthy—wretched. I have seen wretchedness and degradation in almost every form and in almost every land; yet, I do solemnly aver, that I had never seen such concentrated wretchedness as there met my eyes. The worst feature of it was its inertia ; it was the very *inertia* of misery. The people were so utterly prostrated that they could hardly move a finger for their own relief. I went into a little out-building, measuring, I should think, ten feet by fifteen. In that building there were some ten distinct families—not a man among them—women and children. Each family had assigned to it a little bunk made of the rudest boards. Upon the first bunk, lay a woman, apparently in the last stage of lung disease; and with her were two little children, half-naked and helpless. On the next lay another, with her eyes set in death, her hands thrown back, just about to expire in the unconcious-ness of the last stages of typhoid ; and (I never shall forget the horror of the spectacle) a little child vainly seeking sustenance from the dying mother, and that babe evidently uncared for for many hours. On another bunk was a little boy, a bright eyed fellow, with the measles—a disease which of course, would spread itself through the whole company. We were so touched by this scene that we stirred ourselves among the people of the town, and before night had made some arrange-ments for the relief of that wretchedness. But the people then in Nashville, whose hearts were in sympathy with the Govern-ment, were relatively few, and these were overtaxed already in their endeavors to relieve such misery. Let me give you, in one word, a description, more recent, from two very compe-tent agents whom the Commission sent to Nashville early in the present year. This letter is dated the 13th of January, 1865.

" We have spent the day among the Refugees. Their condi-tion is past description. While they are tenderly cared for and looked after, as far as the nature of the case and the means at command admit, yet it is impossible to prevent great suffering.

" First we went to the Children's Hospital,—a nursery of fitty or sixty children, from tender infants to ten or twelve years of age. One had just died ; deaths occur daily, and some days nearly every hour notes the passing of some one of these innocent creatures to his eternal home. A large num-ber of these little ones had really pretty faces, and for a man to look upon them as they lay there, and then think of his own flock of seven, and think what they might, by some adversity, be reduced to, was touching indeed.

"Next, we called on a family living in a tenement of two rooms, both about the size of a common office. It compared favorably in its condition with a Five Points' tenement of the old class. Here lived, or rather stayed, a mother with five daughters and three grandchildren. They had seen days of comfortable living, but now their furniture and bedding were not greater than you would find in the family of a rag-picker of three or four persons.

"We next called at a barrack where we found three hundred persons, mostly women and children. After taking a general survey of this mass of humanity we inquired 'how many could read?' The answer was 'one in twenty.' This must be a mistake we thought, and inquired around—'Can you read?' 'No.' 'You?' 'No.'—and so on to ten, fifteen! twenty! as we passed—not one could read, all of them over twelve years of age.

"As regards personal piety, a good many professed to have a knowledge of the Saviour; say one-third.

"Our next visit was to a family of the better class, occupying two moderate-sized, ground bedrooms; condition of tenement miserable. A family of twelve to fourteen persons lived there—four or five sick—one dead—and several of the sick in a fair way to die.

"We prayed with them, left a trifle of money to bury the dead, and will do more for them by and by.

"Clothing that has been laid off, but which is yet warm and comfortable is greatly needed for the women and children—bedding for all—and delicacies for the sick."

I read a few lines illustrating the state of things existing at Jeffersonville, Indiana, to which point many Refugees have been forwarded during the present winter.

"A short time since, five or six hundred were dumped right upon the dock, in the mud and snow, bare-footed and nearly bare-backed, many of them sick, worn out, and in a most deplorable condition. As a friend was giving us this information, we met the City Marshall, who more than confirmed his statement; said he counted five women in one group without a shoe in the lot, in the snow, until they could be got into an old tent without fire. More or less of them died. Government had now put up a building, in the barrack style. It would hold about one hundred and fifty, as soldiers sleep; could barely cover and keep from freezing for a night, 300; had just got it into shape, had got two stoves, and was getting the bunks up."

Such is a faithful picture, often repeated, of what has met our eyes in visiting these various points of destitution. Of course I do not mean that such utter wretchedness is a uniform and permanent characteristic of the Refugees. Their numbers and their condition, at a given point, are constantly varying; and the Union Commission is doing much for their relief. But just such harrowing scenes have been witnessed a thousand times among them, in the past few months.

Now, who are these people whom we find in this wretched plight? They represent, of course, various classes of Southern society. Very many of them are the families of men who, to-day, are fighting in the service of our country, or who have already laid down their lives for the defence of our flag. Let me illustrate this by one or two cases.

I met in Nashville, a man from East Tennessee, who was enrolled as a private in the army of the Union. He told me his story,—and he was well introduced, so that I have no doubt of the truth of the story:—He and some neighbors, numbering forty, banded together to resist for awhile, in their neighborhood the encroachments of the rebellion. But by-and-by, finding that the rebel army was closing in upon them, they were obliged to betake themselves to the woods, and hide for a long time in caves,—members of their families bringing them food by night. Occasionally one of their number would venture out by day as a scout. If he was taken (and he was very likely to be caught) this alternative was proposed: 'Enlist in the rebel army, or be shot!' And not a man of that band thus taken enlisted; not a man of them would sell his country for his life.—[Applause.] At length, they had reason to suspect that they had been tracked to the caves which were their hiding places, and it was necessary for them to disperse—to escape as they could, one by one. This man made his way to our lines and enlisted; and when I saw him, he had upon him, as I have said, the uniform of the United States. He owned a little farm of twenty acres, upon which he had lived; and when it was ascertained that he had enlisted in the Union army, the wretches went to his house, they made his wife and children come out of it, they set fire to it and burned it to the ground before her eyes, and turned her and her children adrift. She set out upon her weary way of almost two hundred miles, to seek protection within our lines. On that march, she laid one of her children in the grave. She reached Nashville, where her husband was then stationed, barely in time to die in his arms. The poor man had buried her only a day or two before I had the story from his lips. He had three children left. He made arrangements with friends in Nashville to send those children Northward, to be distributed to homes in the West. 'And now,' said he, 'there is nothing between me and my country; I am in for this war to the death.'—[Loud applause.] Shall we not see that the children of such a man have as good a home and as good an education as the nation can give them?

In the upper story of the building in Nashville, which I have already described, which was used as a temporary barrack for the Refugees, there was a woman apparently over sixty, with a daughter of perhaps twenty, and one or two younger children. She told us this story: Her husband was a hatter by trade, living in Georgia. At the outbreak of the rebellion, in consequence of feeble health, he was left for a time unmolested. He was known, however, to be a loyal man. By-and-by, he began to be subjected to stringent surveillance; and finally, early last Spring, he was notified that he must go to one of the hospitals (they accused him of 'shamming' sickness); he must go to one of the hospitals, where they would cure him up, and make him of some use to the Rebel Government. I should have stated that he had three sons, all of whom were conscripted for the rebel ranks. One of them was seized and compelled to serve; the other two made their escape, and are enrolled in our armies. The old man, advised of the design with regard to himself, determined to make his escape; and through the connivance of some old friends, by traveling at night, and hiding in the woods by day, he and his family worked their way along, mostly on foot, till they came to Nashville. The very first office of Christian kindness that my colleague, Dr. Budington, of Brooklyn, performed at Nashville, was a funeral service over the remains of that old man. He barely lived to get within a loyal place of shelter; and he must be buried within an hour, since a corpse could not be left amid that mass of living misery. A few words of prayer and sympathy were all that could be rendered. I afterwards saw the widow, and said to her, 'We will remember you when we return to New York, and see that you and yours are cared for.' 'Oh!' said she, 'I beg you to remember me at the throne of grace.' I learned that she was a sister in the communion of the Methodist Church, and evidently one who knew the grace of God in her heart. Here was a family who had been in comfortable circumstances, a family loyal and true, a family ready to sacrifice blood and life upon the altar of the country, driven out, thus, homeless and outraged, for their fidelity to the Union and to freedom.

Now, these represent a very considerable proportion of the Refugees. I think that, as nearly as we can get at it, thirty per cent. of them at least, are of the class who have been in moderately comfortable circumstances, like this soldier and this aged woman, and of the class who have been unmistakably loyal and devoted to the country.

Then there is another class who have been thrown upon our sympathy, with whom you are all familiar by name: and doubtless many who hear me have had occasion to know something of them, in their observation of Southern society; I refer to those who are known contemptuously as 'poor white trash.'

An intelligent gentleman of Georgia, said to us, 'A great many of the people of this nation have never before known what sort of fellow-citizens they have had in a certain *stratum* of society in this part of the country.' I wish it to be distinctly understood that I am not characterizing Southern society, as a whole; by no means; but I am pointing your attention to a class now brought to the surface by these upheavings of war. If you ask me how far these people are loyal, perhaps the best answer I can give you, is the answer that a bright negro waiter made to our party as we passed through a Western town, when we asked him, 'What are the politics of this town? Are the people here mostly Union and loyal, or are some of them in sympathy with the rebellion?' 'Well,' said he, 'I guess *dey's 'bout ditto.'*—[Laughter.] That is the only answer I can give, and all the responsibility that I am disposed to assume, concerning the class of people of whom I now speak. They are just about '*ditto.*' But I suspect, Mr. President, that you do not need to go to that low *stratum*, in order to find that style of politicians to-day in the nation.—[Great laughter.]

In company with an excellent agent of the Sanitary Commission, after the bloody day of Resaca,—when our party were called to minister to our wounded and dying men for so many hours,—I spent the night in a little hut belonging to one of this class of people. I suspect (though we could not ascertain definitely) that the husband of the woman was in the rebel army. But she was perfectly ignorant of the causes of the war—of what all this cannonading meant. You know of course the style of grammar that prevails down at that level, especially their phrase 'we 'uns' and 'you 'uns'— we ones and you ones. This woman exclaimed, after the roar of cannon and musketry had agitated us for hours, 'I do wish that we 'uns or you 'uns would whip, and stop them terrible cannon!' That was her estimate of the issue involved in the war; and very many of that class of people know scarcely more than that, and care scarcely more than that about these issues. Nor will you blame them when you come to hear presently the statistics that I will give you as to their means of information.

Very many of just that description of people, mostly women and children, come within our lines. Perhaps the husbands have been forced by conscription into the rebel ranks—either by the conscription of violence, or by the conscription of prejudice, or by the conscription of ignorance. Not more than twenty per cent. of the Refugees who come among us are men ; they are women and children ; they are the aged, the infirm, the sick, the weary. Let me read you two or three lines from our agents, setting forth the appearance of these people.

"At Cincinnati we visited in company with Mr. ODIORNE and Mr. STARBUCK, the Refugee Home, Sanitary Rooms, and the Rooms of the Christian Commission ; after that we went to the Barracks, where the Refugees land. These are an old rattle trap, obtained from Government, on short notice, and the only place of shelter that could be had, they are cold and filthy—filled with vermin. They have got the hospital part into a better condition, it is made tight, and thoroughly cleansed from vermin. A description of that class of humanity is too much for me, they nearly all belong to the lowest class of white trash—some exceptions. I will particularize in one family, and they were the best of the lot : When they came a few weeks since, they consisted of the father, mother and ten children, ranging from man and womanhood down to young children. The father died a few days since, the mother we saw lying dead, two children had died— one a (a widow) mother of two children of about four and six years ; another is dead ; another the mother of three children, very sick, *must die*—and the children all sick with measles. The whole family and grandchildren were seventeen. The father of the three last children mentioned is very sick, and will stand more than an even chance to die."

Another agent says :

" Permit me to give you a single case of destitution and suffering which we met at Louisville.

" On Walnut street we called to see a Refugee, from Campbell County, Georgia. She has seven children, and a sick husband. Her children aged from six to nineteen years. She has also one grandchild aged two years. This family of nine persons occupied a room about twelve feet square. As I attempted to enter the room, something from the inside pressed hard against the door. Pressing myself through, I found the obstruction at the door to be the dead body of John, her son, aged about fifteen years. He lay on the floor, his arms and chest bare, without a rag of covering, except the dirty thing

2

called a blanket thrown over the lower part of his naked body. The other children were all sick with the measles, most of them on the floor with their dead brother. I stepped over the dead body, and then over one and another sick one, to speak a word of comfort to the sufferers. There was no bedstead in the room, no table, only three broken chairs.

"Mr. Sedwick, a Baptist brother, with us, said: 'let us sing and then pray.' No, Mr. Sedwick, pray and not sing. Who can sing in such a place as this? This is but one case of many, a little more varied."

Now, I ask you, Mr. President, shall we, before attempting to relieve this misery, stop to discriminate as to the antecedents of these wretched women and children? Shall we not feed them? Shall we not succor them! Shall we not relieve their miseries, and trust that God will soften their hearts, if their hearts have been prejudiced, will enlighten their minds, if they have been duped by ignorance? Yes, I will take this poor, naked, starving boy, no matter who his father was or where he is, I will take him by the hand; I will nurture him; I will clothe him; I will feed him; I will teach him to read; I will teach him the knowledge of God and of Jesus Christ his Saviour; I will teach him that he has a country; I will teach him what he never knew before, the geography of his country, the extent of it; I will teach him what he never knew before, the history of his country, the great name of Washington, and all that is illustrious in our past; and I will *make that boy a patriot!* I will teach him that the men against whom, perhaps, his father, in his ignorance and prejudice and blindness, goaded on by men of infamous deeds, has lifted his hand, are the men who have nurtured and saved and educated and blessed him. And I will sow that land of rebellion thick with these regenerated children. If we are not great enough for that, we are not great enough to be free.—[Great applause.]

But what does this Commission propose to do? First of all, in a word (and I wish to say this with emphasis) the Union Commission *will not take any measures that would tend to pauperize these people.* We guard against that at every point. We must minister to present necessities. We must care for the sick ; we must feed the hungry ; we must clothe the naked. But, in administering your charities and the charities which the people of the nation may commit to our trust, we will guard most carefully against creating a long state of dependence, and holding these people as paupers.

Already, in the second place, we are deporting them to various points where labor is in demand. We have an agent who is now traversing almost weekly, a wide region, from Nashville up through Kentucky, distributing the male Refugees, and such women as are capable of doing housework, where labor is wanted in consequence of the enrollment of the blacks of Kentucky so largely in the army. We are also distributing them extensively both from Nashville and from Cairo, in the States of Illinois and Indiana ; and we have respectfully solicited, and I trust we shall obtain, a full authorization from Congress to the War Department to grant us free transportation in this work of humanity, which at once helps the industry of the country, and relives the Government of the care of these needy people.

But we cannot thus deport and distribute them all. Some of them must be reserved as a *nucleus* for future society in their former homes. They are not all of them by any means adapted to our Northern state of society ; and they love their homes, rude as they were. And with reference to this, we have established at one or two points, and propose, as experience shall suggest, to do it at other points, industrial homes, where the women and the children shall be brought together, and taught to sew, and enabled to maintain themselves. There was an experiment of this kind on a small scale at Nashville, working very successfully. The women were already making enough for their own support, by washing for the soldiers and making various articles for the hospitals, when the Government displaced them and made a requisition for the building as a hospital. But we propose, whenever opportunity offers, to establish temporarily these industrial homes, preparing the Refugees to go back to the portion of the country whence they came, better informed, more intelligent, more useful than before.

But there is a measure beyond this. We look to the temporary occupation of abandoned estates, by such of these people as are able to work, so that they may be enabled to support themselves; and if the Government will grant us the use of any such estates under proper military regulation (for the War Department must be responsible in the case), we offer on our part to take whatever superintendence of the people in respect to education and general improvement, the Government may be pleased to accept or to direct at our hands. In a word, these people must be educated, and helped to become better citizens, and by-and-by be re-established in better homes.

Now all this looks, and with no little confidence, to *re-union*—a re-union of North and South, and such a re-union, I doubt not, as will eventually obliterate the very names 'North' and 'South,' so that we shall have no sections, but ONE COUNTRY, and be one people. I have no question as to the final result on that score. When the armies of the rebellion are broken and scattered, when the leaders are sent forth as fugitives and outlaws upon the face of the earth—such as they have made these unhappy people—we shall have very little difficulty in dealing with the masses that remain. It will of course require time, and a judicious policy to adjust all interests to a proper harmony. But I have not a doubt, that, when our fellow-citizens of the South shall see that the Union is a fact accomplished, they will accept the result of the war, and then, by kindly influences, we will secure their permanent good-will. I have no doubt that we, against whom the South has harbored so many prejudices, will come to be better understood, and in the end truly loved. Yes, sir, we are already conquering in many ways, the prejudices of our Southern fellow-citizens. I met on the field of battle, at Resaca, a brave Tennessean, tall and stalwart, who had been shot through the cheek and jaw, so that every attempt to move his lips caused a gush of blood. He was a loyal man. He was giving his life for the country. As I knelt by his side to minister to his wants, he looked at me with a smile:—'Oh!' said he, 'what a wonderful people you Northern people are! I never had been out of my State before this war; and though I have been loyal and fighting for the flag, I had a great prejudice against the people of the North. But since I have been in this army, and have seen what you do for the soldiers—seen what care you take of them, and the money you pour forth, and the gifts you 'send, I think you are a most wonderful people.' His prejudices were all gone; his heart was rectified. So will it prove also with those who are fighting against us. Ah! sir, we are fighting ourselves into union one with another, and to a better understanding of one another.

I pass on to speak very briefly of the ulterior and more comprehensive objects of this organization. We are dealing temporarily with the Refugees in this ministration of mercy; and for this object alone we ought to have, in the course of the next six weeks—to provide adequately for East Tennessee and West Virginia, and for the Refugees at large—not less than $150,000. Indeed $200,000 could be well expended in this work; and Congress itself ought to help in the matter of seed-corn for the suffering loyalists of Tennessee and Virginia.

But we are looking beyond this. There is to be a work—I will not say of reconstruction, that subject belongs within this hall and the other—there is to be a work of RESUSCITATION. The South is to be revived, to be lifted up; and we stand organized, ready to do whatever the providence of God may indicate in that regard; especially to facilitate, in all kindly and neighborly ways, and by the distribution of correct information—the right kind of emigration, the intermingling of the people of the whole nation; and in the next place, and emphatically, to provide on a broad and intelligent scale for education, assisting our Southern brethren, when restored to fellowship and union, in procuring teachers and in establishing their educational system on a popular basis, corresponding with that which has been so long and so successfully tried at the North.

The radical vice, as you know, of our Southern society, has been in the land-tenure. In the State of New York, taking the cultivated land, farms average 113 acres. In Virginia, with about the same number of acres under cultivation before the war, the farms averaged 340 acres—three times as large as the average in New York. In Louisiana the farms were on an average four times as large as in Massachusetts, taking the same number of acres under cultivation in each State. In Georgia, they average three times as large as in Illinois; in South Carolina four times as large; while in the South there are, or have been many single estates, ranging from 1,000 to 3,000 and even 10,000 acres. A common school system is simply impossible on that scale of land-tenure; and the elevation of the laboring classes is of course impossible. The prime motive to industry, the procuring a home and an interest in the soil, is lacking. The great land-owner cares for nothing save to wring out of his tenantry, be they serfs or slaves, what will best minister to the comfort and luxury of his own family. The war is upheaving that system of society; and these States will be opened now to a productive industry.

The removal of slavery opens the door to industrial emigration and to evangelistic labors. Hitherto the inventive genius of the North could not have play in the South; for men of inventive genius have opinions; and opinions could not be freely uttered there while slavery existed. Such men, therefore, could not find a safe home in the South. *Now, all that is gone.* With the abolition of slavery, every legal, and presently every social obstruction to the education of the masses will have departed. The gospel will have free course and be glorified. Hitherto it has been bound—so that even the ministers of Christ dared not speak in the ears of their fellowmen, nor in the ear of Almighty God in prayer, their abhorrence of that system of iniquity which dominated over everything at the South. The colporteur could not freely distribute the Word of God, nor expound it openly to certain classes. All that will have departed when the grand consummation of the work so auspiciously begun within these halls, shall be reached, and the constitutional amendment shall have been finally ratified. Then, we must enter in with our agencies of education. Let me show you why.

One of our agents being in Alton, Illinois, where was a

prison for rebels, went through it in detail, questioning them
man by man ; and of three hundred rebel prisoners there, how
many could read ? One in twelve ! In another prison, in Saint
Gratiot Street, St. Louis, of two hundred and eighty rebels,
one in seventeen could read ! Among the Refugees who come
in at Cairo (and they have been counted by the hundreds) the
average is about one in twelve. I have already given you an
instance where among three hundred, but one in twenty over
twelve years of age could read. Is it surprising, sir, that, with
that mass of ignorance down in the substratum of Southern
society, the people have been dragooned by their ambitious
and nefarious leaders into striking a blow at a country whose
history they had never read, whose boundaries they never
knew ? Toward such let us have the spirit of the largest
charity. How grand the opportunity that opens before us
now, to build a nation that shall stand, by God's blessing,
through all the ages ; building it on the basis of justice, and
of right ; fortifying it with education, and with all the appli-
ances of Christian civilization.

Do not misunderstand me. Most fully do I accord with the
scope and aim of the measures that it has pleased Congress to
order for justice, under the name, if you choose, of retaliation,
upon the authors of all this crime and misery. Let them
receive the just recompense of their deeds ! But when those
leaders, as I have already said, shall be sent forth unpitied
outcasts, on the wide world, or shut up here to hopeless igno-
miny, we shall have yet another conquest before us at the
South ; the conquest of light—the conquest of love—the conquest of large-heartedness, of free-handedness—in doing good
as we have opportunity. We have another law of retaliation,
that must follow close upon the heel of the law that Congress
has indicated—that Divine law, to be applied to the individual :
" If thine enemy hunger, feed him ; if he thirst, give him drink ;
and in so doing thou shalt heap coals of fire upon his head." .

Sometimes, sir, a great principle is best illustrated to us
when interpreted and verified through personal experience;
and that I may not seem to touch this difficult question without

due reflection, I may be pardoned for drawing my illustration from that source. On the memorable second December, 1859, between the hours of ten and twelve, as I sat alone in my study, I suddenly found it impossible to write, to read, or even to think upon the topic which I had before me. I rose and paced my room for those two hours, absorbed in one thought that seemed pressed upon me from the invisible world. At that hour a brave old man, misdirected in his measures, misguided in his judgment, but grand in his moral heroism, was yielding up his life on the scaffold, for the vain attempt to extricate his fellow-men from slavery. And though from boyhood upward, I had been a hater of that system, and in my poor measure had tried by speech and by pen to contend against it, I there vowed before God that henceforth my life, my time, my speech, my children, my all, should be given to the extermination of slavery from this land.—[Applause.]

When, in 1862, I stood in the prison of old JOHN BROWN, and then went out to the spot where he was hung—my own first-born boy, clad in the uniform of a private soldier of the United States, with his regiment on picket guard at the gate of the Shenandoah Valley—I felt that the vow had been accepted. And when a year later I brought him home from that Valley to lay him in a soldier's grave, I felt that the vow was sealed and ratified in Heaven; and now I am sworn to fulfil it to the end. I must retaliate upon Virginia for all that I and thousands like me have been called to suffer at her hands. Yes, fain would I give to her sons the education, the culture, the influence that they have robbed me of in mine. Fain would I retaliate love for their hate, light for their darkness, the blessings of a Christian civilization for the barbarism that has cursed them, and has cursed all the land. Yes, that soil is to me henceforth sacred soil, to be redeemed for every interest of Christ and of humanity. Thus would I practice toward our enemies in the South this Divine retaliation; thus would I heap upon their heads these coals of heavenly love.

You may have seen the forests of Maine kindled for a clearing, or by accident. The tall flames grapple with mighty trees; they leap from branch to branch; they crackle among the boughs. On they go surging and swelling, a hurricane of fire, till the forest is laid low and all the heavens are aglare, or are hidden by the smoke of the conflagration. Go over that land : it is all one dark, blackened waste. There is no new life there yet. You must now go over it again in detail, and kindle a little fire about every stump and root, and burn it down into the soil. Then put in the ploughshare and you will have beauty and verdure. So when this fiery hurricane of war shall have spent itself, we must go over the track of desolation with these hot coals of Christian love, and lay them down at the very roots of this rebellion. Then all these ashes of hate shall be ploughed deep into the soil, and there shall grow thereafter over all that land nothing but peace and freedom and purity and righteousness. Sir, it is given us to-day to begin to build a nation such as the world never before has seen—reaching out our hands freely in the spirit of fraternal love, when the desolations of war are ended. Liberty and Christianity have lain buried in that Southern land. What is this rocking of the continent to-day, but the earthquake that unseals the sepulchre ? What is this clang of contending armies that wrings agonized hearts, but the trumpet of resurrection calling to a new life ? It is ours to resuscitate the South. It is the work of this Commission and all kindred agencies, there to build, by God's blessing, till we shall see one broad temple of nationality and of freedom covering all this soil— one temple built on the foundation of the apostles and prophets of 1776—cemented now with the blood of thousands of of her native, her adopted and her enfranchized sons—inscribed with the long roll of martyrs, whose rude unlettered tablets mark every battle field from the Susquehanna to the Gulf, from the James to the Missouri—one temple for one people and one continent, purged at last of the vile traffickers in the bodies and the souls of men—consecrated ever more to Freedom and to Justice—the sanctuary of man, the habitation of God. [Loud Applause.]

Speech of Col. Taylor.

Col. N. G. Taylor, of East Tennessee, was next introduced, and said :

Mr. Chairman, it is not my intention, to-night, to consider the purposes of the great National Association in whose behalf this meeting is assembled, but rather to present, to this auditory and the country, facts and reasons in illustration of the necessity for its existence, and its energetic action. Nor, sir, will I assume to review the eloquent address just delivered, either fully to endorse all the views set forth by the distinguished speaker, or to point out any differences that may exist, in matters of opinion, between him and myself. It is enough for me to know that this organization is national and loyal, and charges itself with the alleviation of the sufferings of the unfortunate, whom this war has expatriated, or made destitute at home. It is mine, this evening, to exhibit, as far as I can, the situation of my own particular section of the country, and this task falls more appropriately to me since the war has paralyzed and suspended the civil organization of my State, and there is now in being no constitutional, civil authority, or tribunal, through which the condition of affairs in Tennessee can be presented, either to the Congress or to the people of the United States. We are socially and politically in chaos, and I am glad to have an opportunity, to-night, from the capital of the nation, to lay before Congress and the country, a few facts illustrative of the extremity of suffering to which many of the people of East Tennessee are reduced, and exhibiting the grounds upon which I claim for them prompt and adequate relief at the hands of loyal people, and of the National Congress.

East Tennessee is that portion of the State of Tennessee, lying east of the Cumberland Mountains. It embraces thirty-one large counties, and had a population, in 1860, of about 300,000 persons, of whom 29,000 were slaves, and 3,000 were free negroes.

Almost surrounded by lofty and precipitous mountains, and

penetrated by elevated ridges, running in every direction—it is rich in all the elements of wealth and power, as well as of physical life. For fertility of soil; profuseness of mineral deposits; the elegance and extent of its marble; the capacity of its water-power; the grandeur of its forests; the enchanting loveliness of its ever varying scenery; and the salubrity of its climate, East Tennessee has scarcely a rival on the Continent. Central in position, the blood of the North and the blood of the South mingle in the veins of her people; and it is the crowning glory of this heroic mountain race that in all their history, in war as well as in peace, they have honored the memory of their patriotic sires—by devotion to the Union cemented by their blood; and by loyalty to the Government bequeathed to them in trust. The crack of East Tennessee rifles, on the sides and summit of King's Mountain, was heard in the first struggle for our nationality, while yet Tennessee was wrapped in the swaddling clothes of territorial infancy.

Our fathers "Rallied round the flag," in 1812–15, and bravely fought at Talladega, at Ennuckfa, and the Horse Shoe, and acted a conspicuous part in the memorable defence of New Orleans.

When our own illustrious Jackson throttled treason in 1832–33, and swore "by the Eternal, the Federal Union must be preserved"—to a man our mountain people answered AMEN, and were ready, with their lives, to maintain the Union.

At a later day, though averse to the policy which precipitated the war, when the toscin called to arms in the struggle with Mexico, East Tennessee sent her squadrons to the field afar, and at Monterey, and Verra Cruz, at Cerro Gordo, and around the walls of the city, they breasted the storm of death, and triumphed on the plaza of Mexico.

Thus far, sir, her record is unblemished, her proud escutcheon without a spot. But how shall she meet the trial, and pass through the fiery ordeal of treason and rebellion? Listen and you shall learn. The first scenes in the drama of this stupendous war were enacted at the ballot box. The conspirators put forward a leader, and asked us to make him President. In

Tennessee, although they masked the issues, the people answered, with emphasis, No! and cast a large majority against their candidate.

In February, 1861, the traitors asked for a convention, the people answered No! by 64,000 majority.

Notwithstanding this rebuke, they made the Legislature put the question unmasked, and direct to the people, "Separation or no Separation," "Representation or no Representation in the Confederate Congress," and the vote was had in June. Hitherto argument, persuasion, and promises, and all the artifices of the demagogue, had been employed to bring the people to their plans, but to no purpose. Now the policy was changed, bitter denunciations, terrible threats of confiscation, attainder, imprisonment and death, and a free exhibition of bristling bayonets, in the hands of an organized soldiery, constituted the logic, and gave emphasis to the rhetoric of the conspirators. Armed treason, as it always does, assumed the shape of despotism clothed with terror, holding the rope and the dagger in one hand, and with the other hand pointing, alternately, to the dungeon and the gibbet, and the red blade of the assassin. Our Union leaders, in Middle Tennessee, on the 19th April, 1861, *in the morning*, published an appeal to the National men of the State, exhorting them to be firm and faithful, and to remain true to the Union; that *same evening* terror compelled them, from the steps of the Capitol, at Nashville, to ignore all their patriotic antecedents—swallow the words of their loyal appeal of the morning—and yield their adhesion to the cause of the rebellion.

The people of this section, thus abandoned by their leaders, reluctantly yielded to the storm that howled around them, and the West was engulphed in the pit-fall prepared for it by our faithless and recreant Governor Isham G. Harris. But the people of East Tennessee disregarded alike the promises and the threats, the blandishments and the denunciations, the dungeons and the gibbets of the traitors, and, unawed by bayonets, and by the drilled minions of Harris and his allies, undismayed by the abduction of Virginia, North Carolina, and

Georgia, and by their abandonment in the West—unarmed, isolated and alone—sublimely vindicated their courage and fidelity, by casting 34,000 ballots for the Union, against 7,000 for secession. The State was immediately declared independent, and thenceforward it was treason to speak, write, or do ought against the Confederacy. The freedom of thought, the liberty of speech, were no more, and the Union press was chained. But though we dare not speak, nor write, nor print, we still had *one more vote*, and in August, East Tennessee elected Union men to her Legislature, and chose NELSON, MAYNARD and BRIDGES to represent her people in the Congress. not of the Confederate, but of the United States. Thus, Sir, you see how East Tennessee maintained her fidelity through the first scenes of the struggle. But how has she borne herself in the tragic sequel of the bloody play? Let history answer. Hundreds of her gallant sons sought places in Western regiments at the very opening of the war. [Applause.]

In 1861, our people were disarmed in detail, by military force. Then followed the conscription, placing in the Rebel army all white men from eighteen to thirty-five years of age, and subsequently to forty-five. Thousands of our young men, at once escaped to Kentucky, and consecrated themselves to the service of the Union, while thousands of others hid themselves in our mountain fastnesses, to await the coming of arms and ammunition, with the flag of our country. When, at length the armies of the Government *did* penetrate East Tennessee, many thousands more of our mountain boys, at once threw themselves into the ranks, and are now battling at the front for their country. I said we voted in 1861, thirty-four thousand for the Union. I am recently informed, Sir, by the late Provost-Marshal General of East Tennessee, that of that number, probably more than thirty-thousand have worn the uniform and borne the arms of the United States in this war. The quota of East Tennessee, since 1861, *has always been more than twice full*, and *there has never been a drafted soldier nor a hired substitute in her regiments.* [Loud applause.] If you would know whether our boys are formed of metal

—tough and sharp—and and of the stuff of which heroes are made, let their brilliant deeds at Mill Springs, at Murfreesborough, at Chattanooga, and Chickamauga; in Carter's brilliant raid upon the heart of East Tennessee, in the winter of 1862 from Kentucky; in General Burnside's operations in 1863, in Upper East Tennessee, and at the siege of Knoxville; in Sherman's blazing campaign in Georgia, and battles around Atlanta; in Generals Gillam and Stoneman's campaigns last summer and autumn, in East Tennessee and Virginia; and in a hundred nameless actions, which have sprinkled the whole surface of East Tennessee with blood. Let these answer. And let it not be forgotten, that he to whom the Crescent City bowed her haughty neck, and yielded herself a captive, after he had run the gauntlet of her forts; that he who lashed himself to the mast of his ship, and hurled his fleet like thunderbolts upon the navy of the Rebels in Mobile Bay, and swept them from the sea, or dashed them to the bottom, is a son of East Tennessee, and that FARRAGUT, the first American Vice-Admiral, the peerless naval hero of the war, breathed his first inspiration of patriotic devotion, amid her mountain-girt vales. [Great enthusiasm] Sir, the very soil East Tennessee, from the beetling crags of the White-top mountain, to the battle-scarred summit of Look Out, is henceforth classic ground. Every county has witnessed the conflict of arms, a hundred actions have been fought within her limits, and some of the most memorable battles that history will record were delivered on her bosom. The red sea of war has rolled its fiery billows over all her vallies, and rivulets of blood from her slippery hill sides have swelled the tide of death. Battle-fires have illumined her midnight heavens, from Bristol-on-the-line to the summits of the Cumberland, like the quick, lurid flashings of the tempest. The tramp of cavalry, the clangor of arms, and the solemn thunder of artillery, mingled with the shrieks of the wounded, the yells of charging columns, and the shouts of the victors, have aroused the slumbering echoes in her remotest solitudes. Rosecrans met disaster there, and thousands of brave hearts ceased to beat on the mournful and bloody field. But near the same ground, the hero of twenty victories won back the standard of the goddess of our country, and the modest GRANT led the hosts of freedom to triumph again. [Great applause]

The impetuous SHERMAN, along the slopes of Mission Ridge, leads his tried legions to victory, at the cannon's mouth ; the cool and dauntless THOMAS, with his gallant veterans, flashes terror into the hearts of the foe; but it is reserved for fighting JOE HOOKER, and his splendid corps, following the flight of the American eagle, to scale the steep side of Lookout Mountain, snatch victory from the rebels on its lofty summit, and re-echo in pealing thunders above the clouds, the shouts of triumph from the armies below. [Enthusiastic applause]

But, Sir, this arena of our conflicts and our triumphs has been the theatre of sacrifices and sufferings, at the contemplation of which, humanity shudders and angels might weep.

In peace my people were not rich, nor yet were they poor, but thrifty, industrious, prosperous, and happy. Sixty thousand families, strangers alike to the vices and corruptions of great wealth, and to the temptations and the miseries of hopeless poverty, pursued the avocations, and rejoiced in the blessings of domestic and social life, just as securely and quite as happily as you do here this day. Gently every class of our social organism glided in its own sphere, and every element of our civilization seemed to move harmoniously toward the development of a higher destiny. Aspiring ambition pranced only in the paths prescribed by law. Youth battled with fate for fortune. Middle life, sobered by experience, toiled on, content with competence, till life's evening shadows, lengthening in his path, found him cheerfully waiting to welcome his change. Abundance crowned each passing year. Plenty presided at the family board ; and ever around many a blazing hearthstone, love beamed in eyes that melted at the glance, and bound with silken chords happy hearts that beat responsive each to all the rest. The same roof often sheltered the kindred representatives of three generations, and there the dimpled fingers of playful infancy sported with the silvery locks of cheerful old age.

Halcyon days how suddenly ye have fled! What untold horrors reign where ye once smiled!

Peace bade our happy land farewell. Madness usurped the Southern brain, and treason fired the Southern heart. The conspiracy culminated in war—and war, with his demoniac train, poured out· his garnered fury, blazing with ruin and redolent of death upon our southern homes. East Tennessee would not abandon the Union, nor forswear her allegiance to the National Government. Every failing effort to entangle her in the treason only deepened the gulf between us and the Confederates, and opened wider the floodgates of their wrath. Lifelong friendships, the strongest party affiliations, the holiest church relations, the tenderest ties of affinity and blood, were severed like threads of gossamar. Husbands and wives, fathers and sons, and brothers, were estranged, and became enemies, and every family felt, in all its members, the agony of being divided against itself.

The conspirators hated us malignantly, and yet they feared us. *We* were in the majority, but *they* were in power. The military seized our arms, and, very soon the disarmed majority of the country awakened to find itself in the iron grasp of an armed and drilled minority. Liberty became a myth. Person, property, and life were at the disposal of unscrupulous usurpers.

They denounced coercion, yet coercion was the lever with which they moved forward their cause. They deprecated war, and fired on Sumter. Proclaiming protection, they seized our arms and property. Defying liberty, they fettered our souls, and sealed our lips, and paralyzed the loyal press, and incarcerated thousands of our best citizens, in loathsome dungeons. They anathematized tyranny, and inaugurated a despotism as heartless and crushing as ever disgraced the earth, or blackened the annals of cruelty and crime—a despotism which has shot, hung, assassinated, and executed, by the protracted tortures of half-fed, lingering starvation, thousands of innocent men, whose only crime was loyalty.

The rebel conscription was rigorously enforced. A few of

our Union men were coerced into the rebel army, others were detailed for home service. Many hid themselves in the mountains. Thousands, through great sufferings, and untold perils, escaped to Kentucky, and joined the Union army; while hundreds of others were shot down, or captured and imprisoned, or executed. Our conscripts were hunted by white men first, then by Indians, and then by blood hounds. To be found in arms, or to resist, was instant death, by bullet, bayonet, or rope.

Women '*enciente*' were beaten, and men, stripped bare to the skin, and securely tied with cords, were scourged until until their blood stood in pools.

Five thousand Union men of East Tennessee (it is computed), besides our prisoners of war, have endured the horrors of Southern prisons; of whom, many died of starvation, filth, and vermin. Attorney Gen. Thornburg, Hon. Samuel Pickens, Landon Taylor, Jonathan Bible, Esq., Jordan Jones, and scores of other respectable citizens, many of them aged and influential, fell thus, martyrs to their loyalty.

It is estimated that more than fifteen hundred Union citizens have been *assassinated* or *murdered* in East Tennessee, within the past three years. Fifty-five of this number, I am reliably informed, have been murdered in my native county of Carter. The details of some of these terrible deeds, for diabolical refinement of wickedness and cruelty, are unsurpassed in the calendar of crime. One of my neighbors was seized by a band of Rebel soldiers, on a *freezing day*, and placed on a raw hide, saturated with the water of the tan-vat—astride of his horse—his feet tied tightly under the animal, and compelled, in that situation, to ride nineteen miles. He was then dragged by a rope over his own yard in presence of his family. His house and its contents, including all the wearing apparel of his wife and children, were burned to ashes. Poor Thompson was then lead some distance, tied to a tree as a target, and his body riddled with balls.

Another of my neighbors who had been twelve months a prisoner in 'Libby,' and had just returned to his family, was

3

assailed in his yard by rebel soldiers, and shot dead in the arms of his wife.

Major John McGaughey of Athens, over sixty years old, but in the military service, was recently captured by raiders in the streets of his village. Twenty miles from home, the Major commanding the rebels rode down the line and called for McGaughey. He stepped out from the line, and was ordered to lie down in the road. The officer then detailed five men to murder him, and they instantly obeyed, putting five balls through his body.

But I close this catalogue of bloody horrors, and turn to other horrors as full of gloom. Burnside, whose name will ever be dear to every loyal East Tennessean, lead his gallant army across the Cumberland Mountains, to redeem our land from rebel rule, and to break the yoke that crushed our people. The gratitude that throbbed in breaking hearts, and streamed from tearful eyes, and trembled in thanksgivings to God and that noble army, were the ovation that greeted that gallant chieftan and his veteran host. But alas! the coming of our friends proved but the signal to our foes. You have seen a brilliant meteor shoot along the midnight heavens, rending the vestments of night, usurping in momentary grandeur her sable throne, and suddenly expiring in blacker gloom. Such was the coming of the National army to upper East Tennessee. The brightness of its advent only revealed the hideousness of our misery, and the suddenness of its exit cast a deeper gloom over every loyal home and heart. As the rebels retired before Burnside, capture, pillage, arson, and murder, marked their track. The National forces retaliated on secession property. Ordered to support Rosecrans, Burnside suddenly fell back, the enemy following. The '*lex talionis*' now fell in turn upon the Union people, and the rebels helped themselves. Suddenly our army turned upon the rebels, from Bull's Gap, and drove them beyond the Tennessee line, and then, retiring, left our people again uncovered. Thus, our mountain-bound vallies, since 1863, have been the theatre where hostile armies, like ocean's waves storm-tossed,

have swept forward and back, and often met in full career,
grappling in war's deadliest embrace, and leaving in their
bloody track shallow graves, unburied dead, mutilated death-
stricken wounded, torn banners and exploded guns, broken
blades and battle-shivered implements of death, and worse
than these a desolated country, the smouldering ashes of a
recent prosperity, wasted farms, pillaged houses, devastated
fields, ruined gardens, blackened chimneys, mementos of once
happy homes; and *worst of all*, a loyal population of women
and children and old men, (most of them, the loved ones of
gallant mountain volunteers away at the front with Sherman,
and Thomas, and Gillem, and Stoneman, courting death for
their country), plundered and pillaged of every comfort and
necessary of life, turned homeless and penniless, bare-foot and
in tatters, upon the charities of the country; or left breadless,
to die of famine in desolated homes. Such are the melan-
choly monuments the great rebellion has left all over East
Tennessee.

Relieved last year by generous contributions from the North,
our people, in large part by hand, with hoes and maddocks,
planted crops last spring; and, with a propitious season, cultivated them almost to maturity. But while yet their crops
were in the milk, John Morgan swept down upon them, with
1,800 hungry cavalry from Virginia. After him with rebel
armies followed Wheeler, Vaughn, and Breckenridge succes-
sively, and Gillem, Burrbridge, and Stoneman, with national
forces of cavalry. Thus, since August last, no less than seven
cavalry armies of friends and foes, have swept over and for-
aged upon this already blighted and ruined section.

Who then is surprised again to hear the wail of famine-
struck thousands crying for bread? Sir, while I am talking
here to you, hundreds of tenderly raised intelligent women
and little innocent children, who have never known want
before, and perhaps never saw a professional beggar, are
crowding the refugee homes and stores at Knoxville, who
have left their once happy homes, trudged more than a hundred
miles with unshod weary feet, through snow, and mud, and

ice, clad in threadbare and ragged garments, to escape the persecutions of a malignant foe, and death by destitution and famine.

And yet sir, I would not have you nor the country understand, that I am here a beggar, or the representative of beggars. They who never willingly bowed the neck to the yoke of a cotton oligarchy are too proud, even now, in the deep humiliation of penury, to bend the supple hinges of the knee to Northern brethren, and ask for alms.

Having *one* history, *one* country, a *common* struggle for a *common* destiny, who will deny that we are bound to suffer and to sacrifice *equally* and *alike*, in prosecuting this *common* struggle in the *defence* and *maintainance* of our *common nationality*. But this cruel war for a *common* good has *enriched you* and *cost us* the *sacrifice of all we had*. *Our* ruined homes, on the border, are the *breakwater upon which the rebellion hurled its wrath ; our bosoms*, like rods of steel, *caught the live thunders* of *rebel rengeance* aimed alike at *you*. In the aggregate you have not only *not* sacrificed, but actually *grown rich, you* have not only *not suffered*, upon the whole, but peace, plenty, and prosperity have *brightened all your homes* and *filled your hearts with gladness* and *joy*. You have enjoyed the REWARDS of loyalty. *We* have experienced *its penalties ;* we have *felt* its cost ; *we* have *paid* its *price* in *goods*, and TEARS, and BLOOD. Four years of terrible war find *your* social, ecclesiastical, commercial, industrial, and political systems stronger than ever, moving harmoniously on toward the grander development of a peerless civilization. *In the border-land of East Tennessee, the* war has *demolished all our systems*, and the treason-shivered *elements* of our *organizations* alone *remain*, and civil chaos and civil war, twin sisters, reign supreme.

Then is it arrogance in me, to say, in the name of the loyal sufferers, I represent here to night, in the name of justice, as well as of patriotism and humanity, ' I DEMAND RELIEF for them, at the hands of the *Loyal people* of the North, and at the hands of the *Government?*' What we demand, sir, in the name of our services, and sacrifices, and sufferings, in the name of our battle-torn and still bleeding East Tennessee; in the name of our war-worn soldiers, and of their homeless, and starving, and tattered wives and children; in the name of Christianity and of God, what we demand is *present relief in food, and clothing,* and *shelter,* and *military protection* for ALL OF *East Tennessee*; and PERMANENT *relief,* (in following out the sagacious councils of the President, and of many military leaders who have served and commanded in East Tennessee,) by completing the Railroad connection between Knoxville and the North West. [Applause]

We ask no alms, sir, we seek no gratuities. Side by side with our earnest demands for relief, we present the proofs that we deserve it; and if wantonly or indifferently, our call is unheeded, and the destitute remnant of that most faithful population is permitted to perish of famine; be assured that justice, sooner or later, will send a fearful retribution into the homes and hearts of those who prove callous to her righteous demands.

In conclusion, sir, permit me to add that the sons of every loyal State in the Union are mingled in the history of East Tennessee, as on her bloody fields, where they won their fame. Our vallies and hillsides entomb the remains of the patriots of every State, who died there for their country. Together they fought, united they fell, and the same sod that was enriched by their blood, mingling as it flowed, grows green over the bosoms that rest side by side, in the same grave. They died under the same starry banner, in defence of the same great country, and their brave souls together were heralded to the spirit-world by the loud thunders of battle. No classic urn preserves their dust. No marble monument records their names. But they sleep in East Tennessee's bosom beside her own murdered sons. The maidens of our mountains will plant flowers on their graves, and water them with tears; generations of patriots will honor their memory. The sighing winds of autumn, and the bright waters of our vallies, will murmur their requiem, and our everlasting mountains will sentinel their dust. [Loud applause]

Remarks of Senator Doolittle.

Hon. James R. Doolittle, of Wis., was next introduced. He said :

Mr. President, and ladies and gentlemen :- I have no speech to make ; and if I had had one, I should have forgotten it ; for as I listened to the eloquent remarks of our friends who preceded me, and especially to my eloquent friend from East Tennessee, I have given myself up entirely to think of what he has been saying, and to feel I believe what he has felt. Instead of thinking of making a speech, I have been weeping like a child, shedding tears of sympathy for the people whom he has described. My patriotism, I think, has been very much quickened, as he has pictured the patriotism of that people ; and I have experienced emotions of indignation to which I cannot give utterance, towards those infernal traitors who have brought all this trouble upon the country.

I believe that to East Tennessee we owe as a people, a debt of gratitude that we can never repay—never. Why, to Andrew Johnson, of East Tennessee, we owe a debt of gratitude which his election as Vice-President of the United States does not begin to discharge. I say here, in the presence of Senators and members of Congress, that in the Senate of the United States, Andrew Johnson was the rock on which this rebellion split. It was Andrew Johnson who, in the Senate of the United States, first pronounced the words which no other tongue dared to pronounce in the teeth of those rebels, when they were withdrawing, when he denounced them as *traitors* to the country, and traitors to the Government they had sworn to support.

To that people of East Tennessee, I repeat, we owe a debt of gratitude that we can never repay. And it encourages my heart beyond all measure, when I hear an account given of the devotion of that people to the Union, to the flag of the country, and to its government. Oh ! fellow-citizens, much as we have sacrificed for this glorious country and the glorious constitution under which we live—though we have sent our friends and our brothers to the conflict—though we have been called upon to lay our own first-born children in the soldier's grave, we have suffered nothing and sacrificed nothing, compared with that people of East Tennessee. Let their example quicken our patriotism and nerve our hearts in this struggle. All that men can do, we ought to do to rescue that people, and to repay the debt of gratitude that we owe to them.

While I have listened to the remarks of the eloquent gentleman from Tennessee, I have been shedding tears of indignation as we have had depicted to us, the conduct of those vile rebels who led the South into rebellion against the United States. I have no language in which to express my indignation. I know of no punishment that can be inflicted on this earth that is adequate to the crime of the great leaders of this rebellion. If all the blood and tears that have been poured out in consequence of this crime, could be gathered into one great pool, Jefferson Davis and his Cabinet and his whole Congress could swim in it! On this subject, I feel very much as a chaplain of the army, who left the town where I reside, in the State of Wisconsin, felt and expressed himself when he returned and addressed the people of Racine, in reference to what he had witnessed, and the sufferings which had been brought upon the people, both black and white, by the leaders of this rebellion. He was a very eloquent man, and I had many a time heard him preach. Often to our people, in the kindness of his heart, he had preached the doctrine that men are sufficiently punished in this life for the great crimes of which they are guilty; and that he could not conceive that there could be any such thing as a hell beyond the grave. He went away with our Fourth Regiment; he spent some two or three years in the service, witnessing the horrors that this rebellion had brought upon the people of the country; he looked the rebellion in the face in all its enormity. After this experience, he returned and addressed the people of Racine, and I shall never forget one thing that he said. 'Fellow-citizens of Racine,' said he, 'you know me; you know my profession; you know what has been my religious creed. I have often preached to you that there is no such thing as a hell beyond the grave. But I tell you now, that, since I have been with the army and have seen this rebellion as it is in all its enormity—since I have seen all the suffering and crime and horror that have been brought upon our country by the leaders of this infernal rebellion—I tell you, fellow-citizens, that there is now a hell in my creed for traitors [applause]; I have come to believe in a hell as a military necessity!'—[Laughter and applause.] And after listening to our friend's eloquent description of the sufferings of that people, in my very heart of hearts I do thank God that there is such a thing as infinite justice—that there is a tribunal before which all these men will be brought to answer for their crimes, where their punishment will be just and will be certain.

But I have no speech to make, and I shall not detain you. I will simply state in conclusion my earnest conviction that all that men can do they ought to do to rescue the people of Eastern Tennessee, and to strengthen the hands of all the loyal people who are fleeing from that country to us for protection.—[Applause, during which, the speaker took his seat.]

The Chairman then said: The programme of the meeting contemplates a speech by Gen. J. A. Garfield. The General has made a request that he may be excused. But I cannot find it in my heart to excuse him altogether, and I hope he will at least say a few words.

REMARKS OF GEN. J. A. GARFIELD.

Gen. Garfield then came forward and said:

Mr. Chairman and fellow-citizens:—I will not trespass upon your time this evening further than to say that what has been already so well and so fully said on the great subject before you, has my most hearty approval, in every possible aspect of the case. I know from my own personal experience very much of what has been said concerning Tennessee. It has been my pleasure to be with our army in almost every district of that State; and I know that these things here uttered by our friend from Eastern Tennessee, are true, and that he has not told us the half of the terrible, bloody story.

I heartily concur in the appeal which has been made to you to-night by all these gentlemen who have spoken. I trust that this large-hearted charity that is stretching out its hands from the North, giving, by this organization, every person in all our Northern homes, a chance to exercise his feelings of love and philanthropy toward those destitute regions, will have full scope, and that our people everywhere will assist in the great work.

[The exercises of the evening here closed with the benediction by Rev. Dr. Thompson.]

ORIGIN AND OBJECTS OF THE UNION COMMISSION.

The *American Union Commission*, like the Sanitary and the Christian Commission, has been called into existence by the emergencies of the War. Its work is Relief and Restoration. Thousands whom the war has reduced to want, or has driven from their homes, must now be fed, clothed, and saved alive. As fast as possible, the waste places must be repaired; homes which have been impoverished or demolished, must be restored; and the blessings of industry and of peace must be revived wherever war has spread its desolations. For these objects this Commission is organized.

It is a " *Commission*," having the approval of the President of the United States, and the facilities of the War Department in the prosecution of its work.

It is a " *Union*" Commission, caring for those who, amid the threats and terrors of the Rebellion, have remained faithful to the National Government; and saving for the Country, by timely generosity, the thousands of Refugees whom the tides of war have cast upon our hands.

It is " *American*," because as its object is national, it aims to embrace in one national organization, a work that has heretofore been attempted by local and limited movements, but which belongs to the nation at large.

Already there is opening before us a vast and imperative work of philanthropy, as fast as the theatre of the Rebellion is reclaimed to the Union; and the broad basis of this Commission will enable it to adapt itself to the various industrial, economical, and educational phases of that work which will arise upon the return of Peace. By its fundamental article, approved by the Government at Washington, the Commission "is constituted for the purpose of aiding and co-operating with the people of those portions of the United States which have been desolated and impoverished by the war, in the restoration of their civil and social condition upon the basis of industry, education, freedom, and Christian morality."

In the six months, from October, 1864, to April, 1865— which cover the period of its active organization—the Commission has distributed to Refugees, at various points in the South and the South-West, nearly five hundred barrels of clothing, at an estimated value of $25,000; also, several bales of blankets and cases of shoes. It has appropriated $29,000, in cash, which has been expended for the transportation of Refugees to homes in the West; in providing hospital stores for the sick at Nashville, Cairo, Louisville and other points; and for supplies for the destitute at Charleston. The New England Branch has raised, in addition, upwards of $20,000, chiefly for the relief of suffering Unionists in East Tennessee. By arrangements with the military authorities, the Commission has assumed the care of deserters from the rebel army, who need clothing, and assistance in finding work. It is about to open schools in Charleston, in Savannah, in Memphis, and in other southern cities now redeemed from the rebellion. It has also undertaken to relieve the wants of the loyal people of West Virginia and of East Tennessee, and especially to provide them with the means of raising their crops during the present year. For these purposes the Commission needs at once not less than ONE HUNDRED THOUSAND dollars

The following gentlemen constitute the Commission:

Rev. Jos. P. THOMPSON, D. D., *President.*

Rev. LYMAN ABBOTT, *Corresponding Secretary.*

H. M. PIERCE, Esq., *Recording Secretary.*

A. V. STOUT, Esq., Shoe and Leather Bank, *Treasurer.*

William A. Booth, Esq.
Rev. Wm. Ives Budington, D. D.
Charles Butler, Esq.
Charles C. Colgate, Esq.
David Dows, Esq.
Rev. J. T. Duryea.
E. L. Fancher, Esq.
Wm. G. Lambert, Esq.
Geo. W. Lane, Esq.
A. A. Low, Esq.
Rev. J. McClintock, D. D.
Henry T. Morgan, Esq.
Christopher Robert, Esq.
Samuel B. Schieffelin, Esq.
Rev. S. H. Tyng, Jr.
Rev. H. G. Weston, D. D.

The *New England Refugees' Aid Society* acts as a Branch of the Commission. Its Executive Committee are Hon. Martin Brimmer, Hon. Dwight Foster, Rev. Joseph W. Parker, D.D., Thomas C. Wales, Esq., Hamilton A. Hill, Esq., Henry P. Kidder, Esq., all of Boston..

Contributions from New England may be sent to Henry P. Kidder, Esq., 40 State St., Boston. From other sources, money may be sent to A. V. Stout, Esq., Treasurer, Shoe and Leather Bank, New York, and goods to No. 14 Bible House, New York. T. G. Odiorne, Esq., of Cincinnati, Ohio; and C. N. Shipman, Esq., of Cairo, Ills., are Associate Secretaries of the Commission.